Funny Ribtickleous
and
Funny Ridiculous

Denys Parsons

FUNNY RIBTICKLEOUS
AND
FUNNY RIDICULOUS

Pan Original
Pan Books London and Sydney

First published 1979 by Pan Books Ltd,
Cavaye Place, London SW10 9PG
© Denys Parsons 1979
ISBN 0 330 25905 9

Printed and bound in Great Britain by
Hazell Watson & Viney Ltd, Aylesbury, Bucks

Introduction

Gobfrey Shrdlu, the mischief-maker who lurks at the elbow of harassed journalists and printers, keeps so busy creating hilarious misprints that in three years I have already accumulated enough material for another collection. And it's Shrdlu too who is responsible for those bizarre headlines and anecdotes, such as 'MOUSE BITES CAT' and 'UN-BORN BABY SWALLOWS BULLET' – there's been a plentiful supply of such oddities also.

Gobfrey Shrdlu recommends that to enjoy the items to the full you should read them aloud to the family or friends. Keep surgical thread handy for those who split their sides laughing, and tell them to watch out for the earlier titles in the *Funny Ha Ha* series, which Pan Books keep reprinting.

Funny Ribtickleous

Funny Ridiculous

On board the train, trapped by falls of earth at Wilmington, were 1½ passengers, mostly female.

Express and Echo, Exeter

So far, however, such worries seem premature. The cautious businessman of 1976 seems more inclined to sit on his hands and sprint to the finish line.

Purchasing World

In a statement to the court, Burgess challenged the State Prosecutor to name one person who had died or been made seriously ill by smoking marijuana. He himself had smoked the rug without harm, he said.

Daily Mail

Three times Mr Robert L— tried to get back the 222-year-old violin which he claimed he lent to an aspiring 20-year-old girl musician in 1942. The musician, Miss F— claimed that the instrument was an outright gift with no strings attached.

Evening Standard

Twenty one-year-old Douglas Fairbairn poured a kettle of boiling water over his mother's head, a court was told yesterday, because he believed that his mother had neglected to call the television repair man.

Daily Mirror quoted in *New Statesman's* 'This England'

```
I suffer so much from static elect-
ricity in my clothes and on me that
when I kiss my boyfriend goodnight I
give him violent electric shocks which
run up our noses! There is a definite
crackle and it really hurts. My boy-
friend is beginning to think it's not
worth it.
```

Letter in *Woman's Mirror*

Another statement said: 'Some of the girls went to the bedrooms with the boys.' A third statement by a boy of 15 told how he went to the bedroom to get his coat and found a couple in bed together. It added: 'I could not find my coat so I went to the kitchen, got a breadknife and hit the piano.'

Yorkshire Post

A 30-year-old housewife accused of stealing two tins of meat from a supermarket told Leamington magistrates that she had 'never been the same' since she saw a man running about in the nude. 'I have been under sedatives from a doctor ever since,' she said.

Leamington Morning News

It's all very well for the promoters of new hair fashions who use girls with gorgeous tresses for their ideas, but who cares about birds with lank, thin hair, or those with stiff, straight bristols.

Western Evening Herald

Many diabetic children learn quickly how to give themselves injections. Almost all are skilled in the procedure by the time they are tight.

The Times

After consuming about a hundred portions of chips, 28 pounds of sausages, rolls, ice cream and cake, Mrs Morgan presented the trophies won by the boys.

Classified

I like to be completely independent and feel the only way I can be is to love away from home.

Glasgow Evening Times

He told the bench last week: 'I went to Sutton police station to tell police a stranger had called inquiring about my brother's address. I was wary because my brother was away and I wanted the police to call at my brother's house to check. But the police seemed unwilling to check that the stranger was not someone about to annoy my brother's wife. I think the fact that I manufacture door knobs may have something to do with it.'

Sutton and Cheam Herald

A post-mortem on a parakeet from a council house in Kingsbridge showed that it had died from psittacosis. The bird was bought from a pet shop in the Plymouth area two weeks before it died. Enquiries into its origin have not been finalised because the supplier of the bird is unavailable for comment. He has been bitten by a poisonous snake.

South Devon Journal

An American musician, Eddie Purvis, who was found in a doorway holding a hammer, screwdriver and spanner at 3.50 am on Tuesday told police: 'I was just going to make a guitar.'

Croydon Advertiser

CATTLE PLEASE CLOSE GATE

Notice at Gloucester farm

Shouts of 'whites and Hongkongs (Chinese) go home' echoed through the streets of Port Moresby in Papua, New Guinea, yesterday as crows, spurred by burgeoning nationalism, called for a black revolution and demanded the resignation of Chief Minister Michael Somare's coalition government.

Reuter

* Make your suite reservations now and with our confirmation we will send you a voucher for free dinner for two on your honeymoon (Good for one night only).

Advert for Niagara Falls hotel

Violence between London Transport passengers and against property also occurs, but this study confines itself to violence inflicted on staff at the request of our clients.

Report – *Violence on London Transport*

Rape victims told: Shout 'Fire' – it brings help quicker

Women who are being raped should shout 'Fire!' rather than 'Help,' or 'Rape,' because that's what brings rescuers more quickly, a report claimed yesterday.

The suggestion is based on the experiences of American rape victims, says the annual report of the Rape Counselling and Research Project.

But the idea brought a huffy response from the London Fire Brigade.

A spokesman said: 'We don't think it's a good idea at all. Fire engines are designed to put out fires, not to help ladies in distress. That's a police job.

'If every woman started shouting "Fire" because her honour was threatened it could lead to a lot of confusion. It's just not on.'

Daily Telegraph

About 3½m north west of Tavistock, Collacombe Manor is a fine Elizabethan house with exceptional transomed window, open by appointment.

Shell Guide to England

This Agreement shall commence on the first day of July 1976 (the commencement date) and shall be subject to either party having the right to terminate the Agreement by giving not less than six months prior notice in writing to the other party to expire on 30th June 1978 or at any time thereafter.

Contract between two publishing firms

HORSE GIRL
SUSPENDED BY HEAD

Headline in *Daily Telegraph*

By last week only 700 suspect joints remained unrepaired, but Alyeska has now asked for waivers on the majority of these. The tests show that, while the welds may look defective they would not result in weekend joints.

Guardian

When an order to stop singing is for the birds

Toronto: Birds are permitted to sing for only half-an-hour during the day and no more than 15 minutes at night. That is one of the regulations in a new by-law aimed at curbing noise in the Ontario village of Lakefield.

Now council clerk Earl Cuddie the man responsible for drafting the law, has been flooded with telephone calls from all over Canada. All ask the same question: 'How do you stop birds singing?'

Mr Cuddie ruefully admits: 'I shall have to draw up a new by-law as soon as possible. The council had been complaining about the noise in the village and I guess I drafted the law in such a hurry I just didn't stop to think.'

Sunday Express

DOG RISES WITH THE YEAST

The appetite of a pedigree basset hound called Mary Poppins landed her in the doghouse yesterday. She ate 16 bread rolls and then a loaf left in front of the fire to rise.

But the yeast in 3lb of dough went on rising and the dog expanded like a balloon.

Mrs Jane Burridge, the owner, found her 14-year-old pet lying helpless, legs in air, on the floor of her home in Shipay Lane, Torquay, Devon.

Mary Poppins was taken to a vet who said 'She is going down slowly. There was some concern over pressure being exerted on her heart and lungs.'

Mr Burridge, a staff nurse at a local hospital said: 'Mary's father was a Crufts champion but despite her breeding she has never learned to eat like a lady. She gobbles anything in her path.'

Another hazard is weed killer. If wild growth on road verges looks yellow and dying at a time when it should be flourishing, the council have probably been praying there.

Dog World

Mrs Sinclair's three children, found creaming hysterically by police, were put in care of relatives.

Glasgow Herald

After three days of unloading timber, ripping up floorboards, and sniffing dogs, the battered ship lay hollow and innocent.

Guardian

RACE 3: Amirah Jaya (Razmy) began very slowly with the jockey unbalanced and in the horse's mouth.

Straits Times

Warmest welcome was reserved for Mrs Muriel Wood, 55, who has tried for nearly 30 years to get women admitted. Crowds of men gathered round her, shook her head and said 'Well done, Muriel.'

Daily Mail

SPIDERS' EGGS TALE
GUMS UP YUM SALES
By Our New York Staff

A great bubble gum scandal has burst in America as a result of 'malicious and completely false rumours' about what the makers hope will become the country's most popular gum known as 'Bubble Yum.' The rumours have compelled the manufacturers to hire private detectives to try to identify their origin.

The rumours? That 'Bubble Yum' contains spiders' eggs and can cause cancer. This has led to such bizarre stories as children chewing the gum and later waking up with spiders crawling all over their faces.

The makers, Life Savers Inc., are urging parents to tell children who had been needlessly frightened that the gum was 'clean, wholesome, pure and great fun to chew.'

Daily Telegraph

Hermann Schmidt suffered badly from asthma. Often he was unable to speak and wrote messages on his wall for his girl-friend, dancer Genevieve Becker.

One evening, Genevieve arrived at his house in Philadelphia, USA, and found him dead. He had left this message on a wall: 'Take care of all my belongings. This gives you the authority.' She sent the Philadelphia Registrar of Wills, John Walsh, a photograph of the wall. But he insisted on seeing the original.

So Genevieve and her lawyer cut out an 18in.-square piece of the wall and sent it to him. It was accepted.

Weekend

Enormous crowds of day trippers came to South Shields and found unallowed happiness and recreation on the beach.

Shields Gazette and Shipping Telegraph

He finished at New Brighton with the bunch, but he still has back pains, and he felt every bum in the road.

Observer

● When washing windows, add a small quantity of vinegar to the water. This will keep the flies away as well as cleaning them.

Love Affair

President Nixon's foreign policy adviser, Dr Henry Kissinger, has postponed a visit to Japan, due to tart this weekend.

Evening Gazette, Teesside

FOR SALE: Antique dog basket with 3-kw electric blow heater and log effect, £30.

ABC Weekly Advertiser

Before the Beak

A parrot has been ordered to appear in court in Haifa and sing – so that the magistrates can decide who owns it. A local resident claims he taught the parrot to sing a German nursery rhyme and that the bird was stolen.

Guardian

John Glasser was handed a traffic summons for driving the wrong way along a one-way street in Chicago. An hour later, he received another ticket – for driving the opposite way down the same street. Workmen had put up the one-way sign incorrectly and righted the mistake before Glasser drove up the second time.

Weekend

After viewing the headless, armless, and legless torso, Coroner Marvin Rogers and Coast Guard Captain Willie E. Carr both voiced the opinion that the 65-year-old real estate agent had been slain.

Philadelphia Inquirer

COMPONENT CORPORATIONS OF COMPONENT CORPORATIONS. – If a corporation is a component corporation of an acquiring corporation, under subsection (b) or under this subsection, it shall (except for the purposes of section 742d and section 743a also be a component corporation of the corporation of which such acquiring corporation is a component corporation.

American Revenue Act of 1940

Dusan Vlaco, from Yugoslavia, the second-longest surviving heart transplant patient, has died in Los Angeles. He received the transplant on September 18, 1698.

Bradford Telegraph and Argus

In the early 1970's the Fox Inn was pulled down and re-placed by a pub called The Brush on the corner of Iver Lane. However, after repeated complaints from local residents about the noise, the name of the pub was changed in 1975 to The Coachman's Inn.

Hillingdon Mirror

It is claimed that before Mrs S— used the ointment, the couple had a happy sexual relationship. But afterwards it deteriorated with a loss of fooling on her part.

Daily Express

The committee were told that the city fire brigade officers were issued with nylon drip-dry shorts, with attached collars.

Liverpool Echo

Searched in St Anne's Court, Soho, at 11 p.m. by two policemen, a 17-year-old mother's help had on her a long slim sheath knife. She told the officers: 'I carry it sometimes to sharpen my pencil and sometimes to defend my honour.'

Evening News

Breaking into a house and getting into a bed in which a husband and wife were sleeping was a very dangerous thing to do, said Judge Neville Laski, Recorder of Liverpool, at Liverpool Crown Court.

News of the World

As soon as you know an H-bomb is on the way, said the lecturer, run out and paint your windows with a mixture of whitewash and curdled milk to deflect dangerous rays. Soak your curtains and upholstery with a solution of borax and starch to prevent fire.

Reynolds News

We know that some people are said to have 'green fingers'. I have now followed up these experiments personally, and find that many people with this apparent power have all prayed over their plants and seeds at the time of sowing. I have since been experimenting myself, with similar results. This is indeed an important discovery in the power of prayer.

Letter in *Daily Mail*

They were waving huge colourful flags, somersaulting and going through various difficult movements of the Chinese marital arts.

Straits Times

Seven eggs were hurled at the President's car. He ducked as three smashed into the windscreen of his pullet-proof limousine.

Scottish Daily Express

Since the new signs had been put up at the approaches to the roundabout the traffic had been operating as if it was a roundabout.

Watford Observer

Miss J—, known as 'the Bird Woman of Dinsley Road' was jailed for a week because she refused to stop feeding Judge Dermot Brunning at Liverpool.

Dublin *Evening Herald*

Sir, The change to the use of English in the law reports produced some splendid examples of early franglais. One such was in 1631 at the Salisbury Assizes when, after a verdict unfavourable to him, the prisoner, we are told, 'ject un Brickbat a le justice que narrowly mist'.
Yours faithfully,
P. L. CRILL,
Deputy Bailiff of Jersey,

Letter to *The Times*

Miss Wales cleared because of slap by Pc she kicked

Headline in *Daily Telegraph*

Mrs Pauline Hewitt felt thirsty during the night, reached for her bedside glass of water – and drank her sister's contact lenses.

The insurance company paid out yesterday. Mrs Hewitt, of Wilmslow, Chesire, said later: 'It was so incredible it had to be true.'

Daily Express

Her services were recognised after 25 tears when the management presented a cheque to her.

Nottingham Weekly Post

 DECORATOR
specialises in inferior
work. Immediate attention
Estimates free

Hemel Hempstead Gazette

Her husband, Colonel Camilo Arturo Gay, the camp com-
mander, was also among the 15 people murdered at an
Argentine Army garrison today.

Daily Mail

Withernsea: Lighter winds between N and E brought in
god which kept boats ashore.

Angling Times

A garage in Reading which advertised a £205 Ford Cortina for sale at 10p failed to attract many customers. The man who bought it thought there had been a misprint, but decided to check.

Guardian

<><><><><><><><><><><><><><><><><><><><><><><><>

Three of a kind
Within half an hour a Mrs N. M. Gosling, a Mrs A. G. Goose, and a Mrs L. M. Duck walked into the local show-rooms of the South-eastern Electricity Board in London Road, East Grinstead, to pay their quarterly electricity bills.

Guardian

<><><><><><><><><><><><><><><><><><><><><><><><>

Percy the porcupine felt really needled when he got the brush-off from his three female mates. But he has nursed his punctured ego by courting a broom. Keeper Christine Glazebrook, of Flamingoland Zoo, York says: 'He goes crazy when he sees it.'

Sunday Mirror

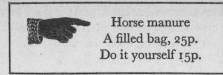

Horse manure
A filled bag, 25p.
Do it yourself 15p.

Sign outside stable

AUDIO/SHORTHAND TYPIST wanted. Leggagig
geggexperigencetoao a LeggggggggfifififikU, e5 oiaiacaa
Legal experience not essential. Good salary and conditions.

Express and Echo, Exeter

Paintings of nudes that are over 50 years old wanted. Tel:
Brighton 687.

Evening Argus

Sheila is the first lady to take over the toast and marma-
lade show, which has always been a male preserve.

Radio Times

The Secretary announced that, as in previous years, there would be a Christmas Eve dinner dance. After discussion it was agreed to hold it on Monday, December 24.

Lancashire golf club report

A Chichester man is campaigning to make the city's public conveniences better places. He was prompted to take action after being on the receiving end of a 'peeping Tom' incident at the Priory Park toilets.

Said Mr. Kevin Booker: 'I think it is absolutely disgusting. 'It should be stamped out completely.'

People avoided using public toilets because of this problem, he said.

He has taken his cause to the city's police and the Chichester District Council.

What he would like to see was a 'loo-patrol' – pensioners, or part-timers, paid to keep a check on the conveniences.

However, said the district's Deputy Engineer, Mr. John Leach: 'If we employed people to sit in the public toilet blocks all the time they were open the cost would be unholy.'

Chichester Observer

From the halls and passages of the evening school in the small Siberian town came the sound of laughter and shuffling feet.

(continued on page 29)

There were only eight days during February without sin, the longest period being 7.5 hours on 4 February.

Rhyl and Prestatyn Gazette

PETS CORNER

**STEAM LOCOMOTIVE, 3½ in gauge,
Pacific type, coal-fired.
Tel: Swansea 578109**

Western Mail

When a South Shields man was found in a car he admitted using keys to get into it, and taking off his socks so that he would not leave fingerprints.

Shields Gazette

At the same time, however, it was clear that both sides wished to avoid a direct navel confrontation in the Gulf of Tonking.

Sunday Telegraph

School records showed very good attendance. The marks of several students indicated them to be excellent scholars.

But it was all a hoax, the Communist Party newspaper Pravda said yesterday. The students were ghosts, the noises mere sound effects, and the records forged.

The newspaper said the imposture in the town of Ob in the Novosibirsk region was carried out by the institution's director and teachers, so the school would fulfil its attendance plan.

It was kept up for a long time in spite of several visits by inspectors investigating rumours that something was amiss, the newspaper said.

When one of them went to the school, he was greeted by the director, Miss Tamar Afanasieva, who ushered them into her office. There they carefully checked the attendance books and progress reports, which were always in perfect order.

'From the third floor where the classes were held came a noise which was obviously connected with an intensive study process,' Pravda said. 'Deafening bells measured one hour after another, and during intervals the hallways buzzed with the noise of feet and the optimistic laughter of young children.'

But it all stopped when the inspectors left. It is true there were some real students there sometimes, the report said, but never more than a few.

As for Miss Afanasieva, Pravda said she told investigators all was justified because the attendance programme should be fulfilled at any cost. Besides, she said her 'pupils' studied diligently, were well disciplined, and easier to teach than real ones. – UPI.

Press agency story

He also says the man 'who likes people, who sings a lot and cries little, who gets up at dawn and goes to bet at dusk' will live to a ripe old age.

Evening Times, Glasgow

Records kept at Stamford Park show that there was unbroken sunshine from dusk till dawn over the holiday period.

Ashton-under-Lyne Reporter

CHEAP AND CHEERFUL OFFICES
TO LET
FROM 1,475 to 7,155 sq ft,
completely redecorated,
carpeted with car parking.

Advert in *The Times*

Mother knew best about the right food to eat, according to a booklet published by the British (providing the protein) and chips (providing carbohydrates) make 'a wonderfully nutritious meal'.

The News, Portsmouth

MOUSE BITES CAT

Percy the cat was in the doghouse yesterday after a mouse he found pinching milk from his saucer bit him on the nose.

The four-year-old brown and cream tom fled mewing from the kitchen, and was later cowering behind a sofa with a tell-tale plaster covering his wound.

'I've nicknamed the mouse Goliath,' said Percy's owner, Mrs Irene Arnot, 61, a councillor at Teignbridge, Devon.

'More than Percy's pride was hurt,' she said at her 16th-century thatched cottage at Shaldon, Devon. 'He streaked off in terror at the assault, and I had to take him to the vet who put a plaster on his nose.'

Daily Telegraph

A 19-year-old Newhaven wife was strangled by her husband only hours after cancelling an appointment with a marriage guidance counsellor, an Old Bailey judge was told on Thursday last week.

Sussex Express

Sign in an Istanbul hotel room, seen by a reader on holiday: 'To call the room service please to open door and call Room Service.'

'Peterborough', *Daily Telegraph*

Another award, the MBE, goes to Mr Harry Kennard of Ivybridge in Devon, for the conversation of the large blue butterfly.

Daily Mail

Don Givens had a chance but O'Leary tickled him and quickly put the ball out of play.

Evening News

WIDOWER, 50s, churchman,
C of E, own home, wishes to
meet widow (similar please)
for fiendship.

Express and Star, Wolverhampton

PRINCESS ALEX OPENS SELETAR RESERVOIR
Princess Alexandra today pressed a little button and unveiled a plague to mark the opening of the new Seletar Reservoir.

Straits Times

For assaulting his wife by striking her with a dog, Alan Kingsworth was yesterday fined £4. It was stated that Kingsworth returned home the worse for drink and demanded his tea. It was not quite ready, and without provocation he got hold of the dog's lead, swung the animal up in the air, and brought it down on his wife's head and shoulders. Mr J Gibson, deputy fiscal, described it as 'a novel type of assault'.

Daily Mirror quoted in *New Statesman*'s 'This England'

Arthur Ramsay, aged 45, a church worker and nurse, who stole four pairs of sheets from an infectious diseases hospital and gave them as wedding presents to two clergymen, was sentenced to six months' imprisonment at Portsmouth Quarter Sessions yesterday.

Manchester paper

You can't put anything over on the hawk-eyed men of the Kalamazoo County Sheriff's department. 'I've just killed my wife,' 76-year-old Floyd Bayes, a devoted husband, told them and indeed they found Mrs Bayes with her head chopped off. Having mulled things over, Lt Larry Chambers disclosed that his detectives have ruled out the possibility of an accident.

Daily Mail

A clanny romp through the Wild West with Frank
Sinatra, Dean Martin, Anita Ekberg, Arsula Undress.

Sunday Times

'The sausages are each about five inches long, and the
contestants will have to eat 24 in ten minutes to equal the
world record.' The Department of the Environment is
being asked to agree to this.

Northern Echo, Darlington

Have you noticed how more and more men are dying their
heir?

Poole and Dorset Herald

The girls are not native to Ireland, unlike the wood pigeons
they so closely resemble, yet they are spreading and multi-
plying at a great rate.

Sunday Press, Dublin

Mr Shields, a resident of Freeland Street, Liverpool, was enjoying the last delicious stretch of a good night's sleep when he heard a loud crash in his kitchen. On reaching the kitchen he found a hole in the roof and a naked man on the floor.

'What am I doing here' the naked man said. 'I come from Burscough.'

Inquiries revealed that the naked man was Police Constable Anthony Richards.

'After night duty I went to a party, 'Constable Richards told his colleagues, 'when I got home I undressed and went to the lavatory. It's outside. I was just about to enter my convenience when three men grabbed me, picked me up, and hurled me through the air on to Mr Shield's roof. Naturally I fell through. There is no truth in the suggestion that I was eaves-dropping.'

Defending the Constable, Miss Ebsworth said: 'Being a policeman Constable Richards could have told the court any number of credible stories. However, he always tells this one.'

Western Daily Press, adapted in *True Stories* by
Christopher Logue

The computer class for nudists, 50 strong, consists of housewives, teachers, doctors, engineers and office workers. Dr R. J. Gibson, club secretary, explained that it is being started partly because the weather is not always suitable for badminton.

Sunday Citizen

But she ran into a storm off the British coast, hit a sandbank in Pevensey Bay and lost her udder.

Belfast Telegraph

At the request of the dog catcher, the council has debated whether or not to employ him on a demand basis. They have also discussed appointing a dog.

Evening Chronicle, Newcastle

'Any sort of erection like this has to be constructed in the proper way or else accidents happen,' he concluded. 'It is quite clear that the sequence of dismantling the bride has not been strictly followed.'

Salisbury and Winchester Journal

Southern Television
programme change.
Delete *Husband of the Year* and insert *Dogsbody*

Agency announcement

When I've filled in my soccer coupon I lay it on a plate and sprinkle a little nutmeg powder on it. Then I leave it for 24 hours before posting it.

Letter in *News of the World*

Three men on holiday entered a bar at Hastings, Sussex. All were strangers and stood around sipping their beer until one suggested a game of darts. The scorer asked each man for his initials and each told him: 'J.S' Amazingly all turned out to be called Jack Smith. The players came from Rye, Sussex; Maidstone, Kent and Croydon, Surrey. For the record, overall winner was Jack Smith.

Weekend

Richard Sheenan enjoys a good show of spring flowers. He eats them.

When he has a pub lunch at this time of the year, he often orders a pint and a bunch of daffs.

Richard, a 53-year-old car-sales manager, of Fleet, Hants, said yesterday: 'I started eating them ten years ago at a rather boring dinner.

'I have eaten them ever since. I love them. They taste sweet and very good.'

At his local, the Fox and Hounds, landlord Ron Kettle said: 'We lay them on for him free. But if it catches on, we might have to make a charge.'

Richard leaves the stalks behind, eating only the blooms. That would be his taste buds, of course.

Daily Mirror

Then one of the newer Labour MPs rushed across the floor to shake a clenched fish in the Prime Minister's face.

Western Mail, Cardiff

This is believed to be the only wild-life park in the north-west. The park is being started by a local farmer, Mr Norman has kept a collection of his family.

Newport and Market Drayton Advertiser

```
           MENU
Fish and chips    60p
1 Piece Fish      45p
Chips and peas    30p
Children          40p
```

Bridlington restaurant menu

A salvo of shots was fired as six burglars played the Last Post.

Ilford Recorder

Worm race

The world's first worm race will wriggle off at Brighton next week: 12 entrants will squirm along a two-foot sheet of glass – to challenge the unofficial world record of 2min. 15sec. Christopher Hudson, of Furze Hill, Hove, trained all the worms and hopes to raise £100 for Oxfam from spectators.

Guardian

The parish council at Kirton, Lincolnshire, has invited villagers to 'help yourself to a gravestone' to tidy up the local cemetery. The disused cemetery, which contains about 500 gravestones dating back hundreds of years, is to be levelled as an open space.

Guardian

Americans won't buy British ginger-nut biscuits because they say the name has sexual connotations, says the Cake and Biscuit Alliance.

Evening Standard

Tel Aviv, March 25
A purse snatcher had his trousers ripped off by his 70-year-old woman victim, a court was told today. He fled into central Tel Aviv in his underpants. –

Reuter

When Councillor Curzon asked whether it would be possible to use various chemicals on the chairman, Alderman Barker replied that these had disadvantages.

Evening Gazette, Middlesbrough

Sandhurst captain-coach Ron Best made it 105 girls for the season yesterday, when he booted 13 goals against Kennington.

Bendigo Advertiser, Australia

25 years ago shoppers rushed to buy pots and pants after Chancellor Sir Stafford Cripps warned that the home market might suffer in the Government's new export drive.

Lancashire Evening Post

Black's Medical Dictionary defines Meniere's disease as: 'A condition in which giddiness, headaches, deafness, and ringing in the ars are associated in sudden attacks.'

Daily Mail

Expensive kiss
John Richards of suburban Worthington, Ohio, forgot to
kiss his wife goodbye when he left home for work. He remem-
bered after starting his car and returned to the house. When
he went outside again, the car was gone.

Guardian

The Royal Opera House management has received a letter
from the Inland Revenue asking for 'the agent's name and/
or permanent address of the following artistes who appeared
during your 1972/73 season: Marius Petipa, Michel Fokine,
Jules Perrot, Georges Roualt, Alexandra Benois and Sophie
Federovich.' Perrot died in 1892, Petipa in 1910 and Fokine
in 1942. The others are also dead.

Guardian

Firemen set off in such a hurry to answer an alarm call at
Ton-y-Pandy, Glamorgan, that they forgot to turn out
the gas under a pan of chips on the fire station stove. They
were called back by radio after a bystander saw smoke
pouring from the building and dialled 999. When they got
back they found that the bystander had broken in and
doused the flames.

Guardian

If it wasn't for those bright sparks who discovered electricity in what is so aptly called the dim and distant past, we'd be watching television by candlelight every night of the week.
Manchester Evening News and Chronicle

A doctor has compiled a list of poisons which children may drink at home.

Ottawa Journal

At Transport House, Islington, Liverpool, this morning there will be a meeting of 220 refrigerated meat lorry drivers.
Daily Telegraph

Mr Rhys Davies, for the prosecution, said that for nearly 150 years the car wavered about in the road before the woman was thrown clear.

Guardian

FULLY FURNISHED HOUSE
3 kitchens, 2 bathrooms,
3 toilets. Suitable students.
£3 per student per wee.

Express and Echo, Exeter

Sir, Surely the most moving prayer for rain is Karel Capek's 'The Gardener's Prayer':

O Lord, grant that it in some way may rain every day, say from about midnight until three o'clock in the morning – but You see, it must be gentle and warm so that it can soak in; grant that at the same time it would not rain on Campion, Alyssum, Helianthemum, Lavender and the others which You in Your infinite wisdom know are drought-loving plants – I will write their names on a bit of paper if You like – and grant that the sun may shine the whole day long, but not everywhere (not for instance, on Spirea, or on Gentian, Plantain-lily or Rhododendron), and not too much; that there be plenty of dew and little wind, enough worms, no plant lice and snails, no mildew, and that once a week a thin liquid manure and guano may fall from Heaven. Amen.

I am, Sir, yours truly,
MALCOLM DYER

Letter in *The Times*

Man Trap
A woman in her sixties woke yesterday to find a man's body jammed in her bedroom window. The man, in his thirties, was trapped when the sash window at the house in Mayall Road, Herne Hill, London, fell. Police believe he may have been a burglar who died from a heart attack.

Guardian

Why pay inflated prices for support tights? A full range of long lasting fashionable varicose veins. Perfects only.

Sunday Express

After being woken from a drunken sleep and asked to leave the home of his wife, a 41-year-old labourer became violet and struck out.

Rhyl Journal and Advertiser

The Post Office is stalling telephones at the rate of one every three seconds.

Sunday Mail, Glasgow

Sterling silver hand engraved locket on sterling silver chain. Locket opens for insertion of two photographers. In presentation box.

Freeman's catalogue

There she lives entirely surrounded by politics and animals – MP father, mother a councillor, three horses, three Great Danes all of whom sleep on her bed (there's also a brother who has given up writing for *Tribune*).

Observer

Sir, It is not too late for Mr P. Owen (July 6) to write again to his insurance company, as follows: having consulted an expert, he now realizes that what came down his chimney and damaged his ornaments were not owls but bats; he apologizes for having made such a silly mistake, and would the company now please pay up, under the 'damage by animals' clause of his policy.

Yours faithfully.

P. B. Soul.

Letter in *The Times*

Folkestone council's publicity committee has put forward proposals for carving a giant smiling face of Mr Heath on the White Cliffs of Dover. Mr Heath, who would be flanked by the faces of Sir Winston Churchill and President Pompidou, would be clearly visible from Calais. 'It would symbolise our unity with Europe,' the council said.

Guardian

Although nearly eight years have passed I still mourn, occasionally, the passing of a Rhode Island Red hen who came to me with a sitting of chicks. Her devotion to me was complete. She knew the sound of my car, and was always eager to meet me every evening. And when I found her in a state of collapse she had been laying large double eggs; she revived for a few seconds to express pleasure in my return, and then died.

Times Literary Supplement

All he asked was a fireside chair and a couple of good boobs.

Cape Times

When the police arrived at the accident, they smelled of alcohol and he was taken to Bury Police Station.

Bury Times

At 10.15 an employee of Gourock Town Council lit the bonfire and in seconds it was a flaming beacon. It was midnight before the last of the burning members were extinguished.

Greenock Telegraph

Presbyterian crossing facilities have also been championed by the Councillor.

County Down Spectator

The house has 3 bedrooms, garage, and good garden. Low rent at present, could be increased. Price with tenants in passion. £5000.

Bordon Herald

Two members of the Middleton Golf Club, County Cork, were playing off the third tee. The low and powerful drive of the winning player knocked the ball over the fairway and into the ear of a donkey standing near the fourth tee.

The donkey stood still. When the players drew near it tossed its head and allowed the ball to come spinning onto the links.

from *True Stories* by Christopher Logue

Will the owner of a grey-coloured goat, which was found in Lea Bridge Road, Clapton, on Wednesday, please contact Hackney police station immediately? It is pointed out that the confined space may not suit the goat.

Advert in *Hackney Gazette*

Widow, 39, height 5ft 8in., 12 stone, would like to acquire loan seven pounds; good security offered.

Advert in *London Weekly Advertiser*

PC Harper found Fenton, a 27-year-old cabinet maker, lying under a bed and wrapped in a blanket. Asked what he was doing, Fenton replied that he always slept under the bed. 'I study economics and the persecution of the coloured people,' he added when arrested.

Kensington Post

The NUM area executive agreed . . . not to hold a ballet
at the county's 24 pits before pressing the case.

Evening Gazette, Middlesbrough

The production was beautifully moved and staged.
Gropings were splendid and the moves were well thought
out.

Evening Echo, Cork

A Circuit Court of Appeals has affirmed a Federal order
that requires US Steel Corporation to drastically reduce by
July 1 the discharge of politicians from its Gary Works into
Lake Michigan.

Houston Post

*Sister Gillian's 'bust clinic' referred to last month was, of course,
'a busy clinic'.*

Berkshire Parish magazine

Two pairs new single sheets, matching pillow cases white
with yellow striped boarders, each £8. Tel: Hoddesdon
435.

Herts paper

At three in the morning a policeman observed a party formed of two men, a woman, and a large alsatian dog, walking down a London street. One of the men carried a ladder, a camera, and a torch.

After a whispered conversation the policeman allowed the party to proceed. They stopped outside a house, waited until the people living on the ground floor finished some interior decorating, then placed the ladder against the sill of a first floor window.

The man with the torch and the camera scaled the ladder; the other man steadied it; the woman with the dog kept watch.

When the man reached the window he flung it open, leapt inside and cried: 'He is here!' Then, turning his torch on the couple in the bed he took a photograph of them – convincing evidence, he hoped, of his wife's adultery. The presiding judge asked to see the photograph.

'I was so excited I forgot to take off the lens cap,' answered the man.

The wife explained that the man with whom she was in bed that night had had all his teeth out that day and she had just made him a bowl of soup.

Granting the divorce the judge said: 'I think the dog was a red herring.'

from *True Stories* by Christopher Logue

The three-tiered wedding cage had been made by the bride.

Somerset County Gazette

Whores in court commonly try to impersonate virgins, and grievous bodily ham suspects often come on like churchwardens.

Sun

FOR SALE, two OFFICE DESKS;
one executive Chair and one
Typist's hair.

Eastern Evening News

HOTEL BURNS

Two hundred guests
escape half glad

Boston Transcript

A Socialist Centre spokesman said the phone call was made by a man with a slight Scottish accident.

Evening Chronicle, Newcastle

Taking a fish for a swim sounds like a fishy story. But for Elizabeth Wright, of Eastbourne, taking her pet goldfish, Horace, for a swim is as natural as a dog lover taking a dog for a walk. And Horace gets his unusual exercise not in his tank but in the sea.

Bobbing along in a special glass bowl, towed by a rowing boat, he gets a chance to see his salt water cousins first hand.

'It's a boring life for a goldfish, just swimming round and round all day,' said 21-year-old Elizabeth. 'So I thought Horace would like to see how the other half lives.'

To protect Horace from the salt water, which would kill him, the bowl is capped and oxygen is pumped in during his weekly half-hour exercise.

'Horace loves the gentle movement and the view,' said Elizabeth. 'It makes him a much happier fish.'

Titbits

Penguin to protest at Antarctic talks

Headline in Australian paper

You can get an answer to any answerable question of fact or information by writing to the Question Editor.

Q. *In what book of the Bible is the proverb: 'God tempers the wind to the shorn lamb'?*

A. It is on both sides of the river; Buda on one side, Pest on the other.

Q. *When and where was King Edward VII of Great Britain born?*

A. Chicago, New York, Philadelphia, Washington DC, and Baltimore, in the order named.

Q. *How much monetary gold and silver is there in the world?*

A. Approximately 1,200.

Q. *Is the claims commission of the United States and Mexico still functioning?*

A. Mixed with melted tar or pitch, it is.

Houston Press

CHEESMAN (nee Maddern).—
(Kristin Fiona), arrived April 25, at Blackwood Hospital, fellow demolition expert for Anthony. Thanks to all in attendance.

     Birth announcement in Australian paper

Happy Sequel to Boy and Girl Courtship
'FLU DELAYS WEDDING'
     Headline in Nebraska paper

Dr Ruth Simon, of the U.S. Geological Survey took boxes of cockroaches to three active California earthquake areas.

'Before an earthquake of small intensity there's a marked increase in the cockroaches' activity,' exulted Dr Simon. 'It's not conclusive, but it's very encouraging.

'If I can do this 100 times, I may be able to convince the scientific community that when these insects have increased amounts of activity, there may be an earthquake.' I trust Dr Simon has kept the film rights.

Telegraph Sunday Magazine

The following are questions put to Zerah Colburn at various times, which have been taken from several sources:

'Give the square of 999,999.' After hesitating a little, he replied 999,998,000,001. He was then asked to multiply the answer twice by 49 and once by 25: a task which he accomplished successfully, though the answer consists of seventeen figures.

'Name the cube root of 413,993,348,677.' To this he gave the correct answer (7453) in five seconds.

'How many times would a coach wheel, 12ft in circumference, turn round in 256 miles, and how many minutes are there in 48 years.' To the first he gave the answer in two seconds (112,640) and to the second before the question could be written down (25,228,800) and added that the number of seconds in the same period was 1,513,728,000. On another occasion he was asked the number of seconds in 2,000 years and gave the answer 63,072,000,000. (These answers do not take account of leap years.)

from *Mental Prodigies* by Fred Barlow

People who suffer from various conditions like Neuritis, Arthritis, Neuralgia, Rheumatic trouble, Colds and many other ailments, can be destroyed without discomfort or loss of time to the patron.

Watertown (S. Dakota) paper

The seats in the vicinity of the bandstand are for the use of ladies. Gentlemen should make use of them only after the former are seated.

Notice in Eastern Ohio park

FOR SALE: to a kind master, full grown, domesticated tigress, goes daily walk untied, and eats flesh from the hand.

Advert in Calcutta paper

DOG IN BED, ASKS DIVORCE

Galveston (Texas) paper

TWO-LEGGED REVOLVER

New York, Monday (AAP): Robert Course, 23, shot himself accidentally in the right leg with a pistol while hunting in the Arizona Desert today.

He decided to fire another shot to attract the attention of his two brothers, hunting nearby.

He drew the pistol out of its holster and – bang! – accidentally shot himself in the other leg. He was in hospital today.

Toowoomba Chronicle, Australia

A 19-year-old girl yak herder in the Everest region has encountered a yeti (abominable snowman), it was reported in Katmandu. The sherpa girl told officials she was knocked unconscious by the yeti, which then killed five yaks by twisting their horns.

Guardian

FLEAS ARE NOT UP TO IT

Copenhagen, December, 10. – The flea circus in Copenhagen's famed Tivoli Gardens has been forced to close because of a shortage of 'actors.'

Manageress Else Torp said increased hygiene had made it impossible to find enough fleas that live off humans.

Ordinary dog fleas could not be trained to perform, she added.

The flea circus was one of the main sideshow attractions in the Tivoli, and was believed the only one in Europe.

Reuter

The annual Christmas party at the Ashley Street school was hell yesterday afternoon.

Springfield (Mass.) paper

John Benson, who was run down at the same time, died of his injuries. Last night his temperature declined somewhat.

Wilkes-Barre Record

To ascertain whether your mouth is in proportion to your whole face, take a knitting needle and hold it vertically so that it passes through the centre of your eye (as you look straight ahead) and reaches down to your chin.

Modes et Travaux

We learn with pleasure of the birth of a son to Mme and M. Gaspard Damien, the genial centre back of the sports association. Our sincere compliments to the happy parents, in particular to M. Mathieu, treasurer of the club.

Ouest-France

The Misses Doris, Agnes and Vivian Smith are spending several days at the home of their mother, Mrs W. L. Lawrence. This is the first time that the community has had the pleasure of seeing the Smith girls in the altogether at one time.

Sidney Daily News, Ohio

SPOTTED MAN WANTED FOR QUESTIONING

Hackney Gazette

Yes, Man DOES Bite Dog

A special award for dusting off clichés to Mr François Moulders, who intervened in a fight between his dog and another last July in Blankenberge, Belgium. The way Mr Moulders intervened was to seize his pet's opponent, a four year old setter called Pilou, and bite her. He bit her repeatedly until Pilou's owner hit him with her handbag. Mr Moulders was let off with a caution, and a rabies shot.

Telegraph Sunday Magazine

To New York detectives Victor Ruggiero and Frank Iaimundi who, while fruitlessly searching a house, discovered ten thousand pounds' worth of 50 dollar bills baked into a dish of pasta. What interested the courtroom was whether the discovery was the result of deduction or appetite?

'Had it not been for the fact that this was the fattest looking pan of lasagne we ever saw, we might have come away empty handed,' Iaimundi said, ambiguously.

Telegraph Sunday Magazine

Houchin also killed a doe on his hunting trip. He was accompanied by Paul Smith, who bagged a doe and a buck, and by Mrs Bob Smith, mother of the latter.

Prescott (Arizona) paper

Notice is given fixing the charge for the use of the WC at the zoo in the Bois de Vincennes at 3 francs. This new tariff will take effect retrospectively as from 1 July last.

Notice at Vincennes

He is the son of the ancient principal of our college who, behind his thick glasses, hid a heart of gold.

Courrier de Saône-et-Loire

Tho retired now from active mission work, he is 'doing the work of the Lord on the side' while following his earlier and more respectable trade as a boss bricklayer.

Washington Star

The Game Commission of Pennsylvania has made a thorough review of the mammas of Pennsylvania and finds that there are more than fifty species.

Clarion Democrat, Pennsylvania

When Lily Stonefield gave evidence in an Australian court against a bag-snatcher, she identified the exhibit produced as the bag stolen from her.

She also identified its contents, which included: A purse containing 16s 9d, a box of face powder, a lipstick, a compact a comb, a bottle of hair spray, a toothbrush, a tube of tooth-paste, a dozen hair-grips, two handkerchiefs, a pair of gloves, a diary, an address book, a pair of silk panties, an apple, a bag of fruit pastilles, a cheese sandwich, a ballpoint pen, two pencils, a manicure set, two bracelets, three rings, a neck-lace, a pair of nylons, a small mirror, a shoe horn, a pair of knitting needles, a knitting instruction leaflet, a golf ball, a typewriter ribbon, an empty cigarette carton, a box of matches, a collapsible coathanger, two clothes pegs, a tin of throat lozenges, a reel of cotton with two needles attached, 18in of elastic, a 7in zip fastener and – laughter in court – a miniature copy of Charles Dickens' *Old Curiosity Shop*.

Titbits

To Ms Sharon Mitchell, heroine, if that is the word, of the X-rated *Captain Lust*, who was having trouble cashing a cheque at a New York bank because she was not carrying a driver's licence or any other documentation.

She was, happily, carrying a girly magazine wherein she appeared in the nude. She handed over the magazine, hitched her sweater up to her chin, and arranged herself in the same pose.

Yes, they cashed her cheque.

Telegraph Sunday Magazine

A daughter, Thurile Louise, was born on 12 March to Mrs Harry Emsworth at the special town meeting.

Lewiston (Maine) paper

A paperhanger and a building-repair man testified that they had seen him slay his wife – once when he became enraged over finding a shirt unlaundered and again over a necktie.

Pottstown News, Pennsylvania

Quadruplets – all girls – were born yesterday to Mr and Mrs tense heat and so spent several hours flying over Gibraltar, northern Africa and southern Spain.

Wenatchee (Washington) paper

Infantry Mounted Officer's bride, complete, $35.

Toronto Mail and Empire

An interesting marriage was celebrated on September 21 in the Roupell Park Wesleyan Church, the first that has taken suede gloves and they carried rustic baskets of moss and place in that edifice between Mr Louis Donald and Miss Armitage.

Lady's Pictorial

When Roy Swaby took a bath he could lie back and study the stars if the weather was good. If not he had to use his umbrella. Roy, of Newham, London, built a bathroom extension on his house without getting planning permission. When the council surveyor eventually came to inspect it, he said: 'I'm afraid the roof will have to come off.'

Despite its twin sinks, shower and modern toilet the bathroom did not comform to building regulations. But without a roof it ceased to be a room in law. So Roy took the roof off, and had the first open-air bathroom in Newham.

Weekend

SHOT FIRED AS PILOT WAVED AT NUDE WIFE

A woman told a court in Durban yesterday that a hangglider pilot flew over and made a sexual suggestion as she was sunbathing nude on the roof of her garage.

Mrs Loran Thompson was giving evidence in the trial of her husband, Francis Thompson, 68, who denies the attempted murder of two hang-glider pilots by firing at them with an air rifle. She said she had complained to police many times about the activities of hang-gliders.

When one flew past the window and waved as the family were lunching her husband went for a gun but he did not shoot at the pilot, Mrs Thompson said. The trial was later adjourned.

Reuter

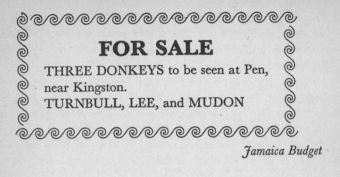

FOR SALE

THREE DONKEYS to be seen at Pen, near Kingston.
TURNBULL, LEE, and MUDON

Jamaica Budget

The procession was very fine, and nearly two miles in length, as was also the sermon of the minister.

New York Times

More than 150 were believed killed, many villages and towns were devastated, hundreds of peanuts made homeless.

Richmond Palladium, Indiana

3.10 Questions to the Prime Minister. Love from the House of Commons.

Express and Star, Wolverhampton

The road forms the last link in a completely restructured one-way traffic system in the city centre, which is designed to improve traffic flow and ease congestion on the overused River Severn bridge.

Police are standing by today to cope with expected traffic jams.

Birmingham Post

Correction

A major ingredient was omitted in the recipe for Gingerbread Puzzle cookies, printed in yesterday's Gazette.

There should be $2\frac{3}{4}$ cups all-purpose flour.

Montreal Gazette

Hongkong, October 16 (Special). – Chinese newspaper editors here were baffled by the report of the insult hurled at the Australian Prime Minister (Mr Holt) in Parliament – 'dirty low mug.'

It was a tricky task to translate the rich Australian idiom into Cantonese which could then be properly converted into written Chinese characters without losing the poetic sense of the original.

They finally settled for 'Lapsop – Lan – Situng' which means roughly 'garbage-crawling insect-bedroom utensil.'

There was no attempt to evolve a Mandarin translation.

One editor said: 'Mandarin is a dignified language. The Cantonese dialect is much dirtier and more expressive – like Australian.'

Courier Mail, Australia

Preacher next Sunday: Rev. J. Nicholas. 'Why worry? It may never happen'.

Church notice

The only living thing aboard the hulk is the ship's cat, which obstinately refuses to move. So far no unlucky shell has pentrated to her engine room and this portion of her is in perfect condition.

Canadian paper

Mrs Jessup was so clearly the master in the first five games of the singles match that the event began to take on the attributes of a complete rout. Miss Palfrey was obviously nervous and her shoes were not coming off successfully.

New York *Herald Tribune*

Ducking under crossing gates and running behind a westbound freight train, an electric passenger train which he was trying to catch struck and mangled Henry Rasku of 122 Lockman Avenue today.

Evening Post, New York

PART-TIME JOB

An unexpected vacancy for a knife-thrower's assistant. Rehearsals start immediately in preparation for Milton Keynes City Show. July 23-24.
Please apply in writing to the city show office.
BLACK HORSE LODGE
Linford, Milton Keynes

Advert in *Bedfordshire Times*

A man, aged 29, fell 100ft. down a factory chimney and battered his way out through the brickwork after being trapped for 12 hours. Mr Andrew Reid said at Bury General Hospital, Lancashire, that he had been curious to see what the town looked like from the top of the chimney at New Bury Paper Mills, where he works.

Guardian

Embarrassed BBC television officials admitted last night that their exclusive film of the Loch Ness monster, was in fact, a duck.

Daily Telegraph

If not convenient to move furniture outdoors to clean, place a damp cloth over the piece of furniture and then beat it.

Atlanta Journal

Higgins, of Selby Road, Annerly, was found guilty of unlawfully possessing a cutlass. He also admitted harassing Miss Ivy Parton by removing her kitchen sink and water closet.

Sun

Joan, who lives in Croydon, Surrey, and has a collection of 3000 wrapped sugar lumps, wants to see the world divided into five sections.

Northern Mirror

WINDHOEK (South-West Africa). A villager became so angry when he thought his girl friend was hiding from him in a house that he hijacked a nine ton mechanical shovel and knocked down the prefabricated building. She was not there.

Express

THE ULTIMATE IN CUSTOMER SERVICE?

Joe Moran, Passenger Officer at JFK, has the answer.

Last week, 400 passengers from London arrived at JFK on flight 501. In Customs an announcement was made that there would be a delay in baggage delivery due to an obstruction on the baggage belt.

An elderly man from the flight approached Joe and said, 'Excuse me, while I'm waiting for my bag could you direct me to the men's room?' A few minutes later the man returned smiling and said to Joe, 'Thank you, I got my bag.' Confused, Joe said, 'How did you find your bag? We're having trouble with our baggage belt and the luggage hasn't . . .' 'Well,' the old man said, 'I was standing in the men's room and the bag fell through the ceiling and landed right at my feet. This is the best service I've ever had.'

British Airways Staff Magazine

FARM PROTEST: Farmers are threatening legal action over damage which, they claim, was caused by a 'save the countryside' walk, at Bicester. They say that hundreds of walkers trampled over fields and left litter in ditches and hedgerows.

Guardian

If you haven't already listened to the enclosed demonstration record with the voice of Alvar Lidell, play it now to hear how faithfully we have reproduced the authentic big band sound – but without the scratchiness of the old 78s, which we have simulated on this record by electronic means to approximate the sound you'd hear if you played the original.

Time-Life Records

My mention the other day of an Irish hotel where a door marked 'Switchroom' separated the lavatories for men and women has reminded one reader of a research department in a local factory. At the end of a corridor, apparently, were three doors marked 'Ladies', 'Gentlemen' and 'Experimental'.

'Peterborough', *Daily Telegraph*

The 150 women members of the Queensland flute guild were asked not to wear backless dresses at the Brisbane Conservatorium of Music concert.

'Please wear high-back dresses,' pleaded their president, James Carson. Asked why, he said: 'We want to pin sheet music on their backs. They can come frontless but not backless.'

Sheffield Star

The mugger was so humiliated at being 'put out for the count' by a woman that he threw his glass eye at police when he appeared at court later.

South Wales Echo

He had been eating tomatoes and drinking milk, and the woman may have mistaken this as an offer for sex. It was not, he said.

Rhodesia Herald

In an ordinary newspaper column there are 10,000 letters and there are seven wrong positions for each letter, making 70,000 chances to make errors and several million chances for transpositions. Next, consider the number of columns in each paper. Then you can readily see the chances for mistakes.

Did you know that in this sentence: 'To be or not to be', by transposition above, 2,759,022 errors can be made? Now aren't you sorry you got mad about that little mistake last week?

Dubuque Witness, Iowa

Mr Evans claimed the light was green but he was found guilty of failing to obey traffic lights and was fined £15. Mrs Rose Evans told the magistrates the light was blue. She was given an eye test.

Kingston Borough News

His angling exploits were once rewarded when the Mayor presented him with an inscribed manhole cover for catching three large tunny fish.

Sheffield Morning Telegraph

Following the arrest customs agents began a thorough search of the freighter. At 10.30 am three more plastic bags were seen gloating near the ship and the police harbor patrol was summoned.

Two bags were picked up near the pier by a harbor patrol motor boat. The third was found gloating 500 feet away by a Coast Guard launch.

Philadelphia Inquirer

DID YOU KNOW?
The first Boy Scout troop in Vermont was organised in Vermont.

Middlebury Independent

'I feel comme ci, comme ca – which means I feel he was better in the Justice Department than he would be in the Citizens for Nixon,' Mrs Mitchell said.

New York Times

Eugene Kisamore of Flintstone, who said he heard a large flock of geese flying over his area, headed almost due east about 9.40 pm yesterday.

Cumberland News, Maryland

He said the marriage between Violet Knowles and Stewart had been ill-fated. Everything bought for the marriage was bought by Violet Knowles. The only things supplied by Stewart were a tea caddy and a road roller.

Winsford Chronicle

*   *   *

We are asked to state that Sheila Doris Fenton and John Morris, who were named as the victims of an assault in the report of a case at Birmingham Assizes this week, were not the same Miss Fenton and Mr Morris named in a different context later in the same report.

Coventry Evening Telegraph

*   *   *

A man has complained to the National Health Service Executive Council for Glasgow that he left his false teeth in a left-luggage office in a city station, but when he went back to collect them the station had been demolished.

Glasgow Evening Citizen

Admittedly, a lot of arm waving has gone over the dam
since then.

Science

Daventry Development Committee are looking for two
pretty girls to show off their expansion regions.

Northampton Chronicle and Echo

A small fire in a coal shed at 4 Mansfield Road, Bamford,
was put out by firemen on Wednesday. Mrs M. Stephan
was the pianist.

Rochdale Observer

'LEONORE' ONLY OPERA
BEETHOVEN WROTE ON
MONDAY EVENING

San Antonio Express, Texas

Cheats (Inc.) prosper

Toronto, December 16

The old custom of cheating in university essays has become a big business in the United States. Last year companies selling essays made about $250,000 (about £104,000) and now they are planning to expand into Canada. One company is training men to manage offices in Toronto, Montreal, and Vancouver, and another is installing a free telephone system for students to order essays from anywhere in North America.

Essays produced under non-examination conditions generally count in North American universities towards a final degree, and education officials say that if the practice of buying essays is allowed to continue a college degree will become increasingly less credible as a certification of academic competence.

In the United States last year the leading essay houses sold more than 10,000 papers. Mr Bill Carmody, who runs the oldest and largest such firm, International Termpapers Incorporated, has built a file of more than 80,000 essays. He has a staff of over four hundred freelance writers who write for a fee of between 20p and 40p a page. Mr Carmody sells copies for £1 a page.

Guardian

Rev A.J. and Mrs Prosser say they had a dandy time out at their place last Thursday when 55 Baptist clergyman each with 35 wives broke in on them for a picnic.

Nova Scotia paper

Ricci's Gerard Pipart suddenly likes pears with everything. They give clothes a sexy softness.

New Hampshire paper

The key shot in Jacklin's round was an eagle two on the 383-yard 4th hole. He hit a 6-iron 160 yards past the cup and the backspin caused the ball to back up into the hole.

Chicago Tribune

Dealers reported to the Reserve Bank that the range of interest rates paid during the week for loans at call was from 1 per cent to 6.5 per cent and for loans for fixed periods from 92 to 113 miles an hour.

Australian Financial Review

Instant elephants

JOHANNESBURG, Sat. – An elephant goes into one end of a new machine and comes out the other as cut-lunches for African miners.

The Africans get their elephant–burgers all neatly packed.

The machine is being used at the Kruger National Park, South Africa's famous game reserve.

The machine gets through an elephant a day, turning out seven tons of lunches.

The tusks and hides are sold, and the bone used for meal.

Toowoomba Chronicle, Australia

An Ashgrove man says it happened when a fellow radio 'ham' was talking to an operator in Britain.

Both were using a new-fangled electronic 'vox' device which automatically turns on the transmitter when the operator speaks instead of his having to press a button.

The Aussie operator was talking when his dog came into the transmitting shack and began to bark. Sure enough, back over the 12,000 odd miles came the sound of the British operator's dog barking back. Pretty soon the harassed 'hams' were in in the middle of the first international dog fight.

Toowoomba Chronicle, Australia

Big-time commodity speculator and small-time investor began to gamble on silver futures. That seemed a minimal risk because the world produces far less silver than it uses.

Time

8.30 pm. Free CBC concert. Mary Morrison, soprano, with Viola da Gamba, harpsicord.

Toronto Citizen

Brisk crosswords forced cancellation of the second round of the Olympic team ski-jump elimination tournament at Pine Mountain slide.

Chicago Sun-Times

In spite of the snags that bedevil every big exhibition the British Museum's spectacular display of gold and silver dating from AD300 to 700 opens on schedule tomorrow under the title 'Wealth of the Roman World'.

Preparations for handling crows of Tutankhamun dimensions were well in hand yesterday.

The Times

ROME – Maria Marcon, 24, told police Tuesday she accepted a ride from a dark-haired stranger and was robbed by a three-foot dwarf who popped out of a cardboard box on the back-seat.

Regina Leader-Post

A successful coffee morning was held at the Manse, Carmarthen Road, Swansea. Film strips were shown of topical interest, especially shots of the previous year's coffee morning.

Congregational Monthly

OKLAHOMA CITY – Harold Arnold, a watchman, deposited 35 cents in a City Hall vending machine and reached in to get a sandwich. When the machine caught his hand, he pulled out his pistol and shot the machine twice. The second shot severed some wires and he got his hand out.

New York Times

When two men stole six sheep from a farm at Mundford, they found that they could only get five of them in the back of their van. So the other one had to sit in the cab between the two men. But the men had to pass through Watton on their way home. They feared the sheep sitting in the cab would be conspicuous so they 'disguised' it by putting a trilby on its head.

Eastern Evening News

Ex-Southport F.C. chief, Billy Bingham, was to be seen putting his team Everton through their paces on Ainsdale beach earlier in the week. A meeting of toads has been called to discuss the problem.

Southport and District Advertiser

The traffic which was blocked was confined mostly to golfers and boasters.

Ithaca Journal, New York

The buttons button higher to allow the chest to become in red poppy, plum, spinach, instant coffee and filtered pagoda-style as a friendly gesture to China.

San Francisco Chronicle

His father was a ne' er-do-wall house painter.

Washington Star

FRIGHTENING FACTS. A warning on declining U.S. naval power is contained in this issue of *Jane's Fighting Ships*, an annual compendium of the world's navies published in London. The editor of this authoritative publication comments: 'The grated onion and a dash of Worcestershire sauce give the extra "zing" party-goers love.'

Canaan Connecticut Western

Mr Day knows something about coins. He claims his own collection is worth more than £380. If he had a certain penny and a certain half-crown he reckons it would be worth £25,000.

Sevenoaks Chronicle

GIRL LOBSTERS NEED
A PROTECTED PUBERTY
Headline in *Daily Telegraph*

Arthur S— was looking forward to his salmon sandwich on his way back from washing his hands. But he found his father had got there first so Arthur shot him in the groin.

Leicester Mercury

Mr Spalding believed that the secret of his eternal youth lay in the fact that he had an early morning skipping session followed by a long walk every day. The funeral takes place next Tuesday.

Kentish Times

A 21-year-old farmer who left his car to look at a carpet snake he had run over near Ingham was bitten by the snake and knocked down by a car.

Canberra Times

SAN FRANCISCO (AP) – There is a business structure here that is .34 feet long, houses an industrial design firm, and once collided with a Navy submarine.

St Louis Post-Dispatch

Not all of those cars recalled had defects. For instance; General Motors recalled 32,640 Buicks, Oldsmobiles and Pontiacs to find 1,250 which had been fitted with wheels.

Vancouver Sun

Q. *Was the horse's blood-drenched head in* The Godfather *from a real horse?*
A. Yes. 'We attempted to use a taxidermist's head but it didn't look right,' producer Al Ruddy's spokesman informs.

Plain Dealer Magazine

SINGAPORE (AP) – Customs officials have seized more than 10,500 nude calendars brought into the country since last November, nude art authorities announced.

New York Times

The guest artist is a native of Boston but currently lives in Paris where she was decorated as Chevalier des Arts et Lettres in 1962 and as Chevalier de la Legion d'Horreur in 1966.

Norfolk Virginian-Pilot

Miss Carton said Mr Smithers was driving with his left arm along the back of the seat, and although it may have appeared to the police that she was resting her head on his chest, she was in fact looking for a sponge under the dashboard in order to clean the screen.

Hampshire Telegraph

In her statement the girl said that he had put his hand on her chest and a guinea pig which she had under her jumper had bitten him.

Cannock Advertiser

Two men found outside a Willenhall factory with a sledge-hammer, a torch, and a pair of gloves told a policeman: 'We are meeting two girl friends,' Walsall magistrates heard today.

Birmingham Mail

A young doctor, who ran from his home and attacked a woman, breaking her wrist, told the police that he thought the woman was his wife.

Daily Express

WANTED – Women, Evening shift, 5.30 to 9.30, for Backwashing, Regilling, and Tophat Minding.

Advert in *Bradford Telegraph and Argus*

Focus on Sweden

Mildred Carpon continues her journey through Portugal.

Providence Journal, Rhode Island

Within seconds a little black bus operated by a policeman that looked like a City of Ithaca transient bus pulled up.

Ithaca Journal, New York

The three men were allegedly involved in a mock duel with home made words in front of the Liquor Store in Main Street.

Virgin Islands paper

In a piano recital at the Richland School auditorium last week, presented by Mrs Eula Bedgood's pupils, four murders on the programe were inadvertently omitted from the story published in last week's issue of the Journal.

Richland Journal, Georgia

Q. *I have a football helmet, in good condition, that dates drum with a screen on top. Everybody around me is doing it. I have a steel drum.*

A. No, it is illegal. Garbage and trash collection are available in your area.

Fort Myers News-Press, Florida

All restrictions of entertainment in Falkirk public bars are to be lifted for the next three months until new by-laws are drawn up, the magistrates decided yesterday at a special meeting. The action followed a complaint last week by William K—, the Provost, who said a go-go dancer, dressed in a bikini, put his spectacles inside her panties.

Glasgow Herald

A chance remark made by Funeral Director Mr David Wells at Leighton and Linslade Chamber of Trade and Commerce may result in 100 tons of cod heads being delivered to his home.

Beds and Bucks Observer

Three hundred dangerous drugs are missing at Batheaston. They were taken from a dog kennel. Also missing from the kennel were 36 holiday colour slides.

Bath and Wilts Chronicle

Vera Czermak jumped out of her third-storey window when she learned that her husband had betrayed her. Mrs Czermak is recovering in hospital after landing on her husband, who was killed.

Chicago Daily News

Do not wash the plastic ear pieces of your stethoscope with fragrant, floral scented soaps. If you do, bees will fly in your ears looking for honey.

New England Journal of Medicine

DRIVER OF DEATH CAR HELD
ON SUSPICION OF NEGLIGIBLE HOMICIDE

California paper

Former prominent New Yorker had liver in Paris for eight years.

New York Evening Post

MORE MEN FOUND WEDDED THAN WOMEN

Washington Star

The Sunbeam Band of Central Baptist Church, meeting at ten o'clock at the church where transportation will be provided to a picnic which will be hell in the country.

Kentucky paper

Once again we would like to thank Mr Trevor Till for his continuing help in cutting the churchyard grass. It is also nice to see so many people tidying up their own graves and the space around them.

Thornbury and District Church Magazine

The letter, which was read by the magistrate, Mr John Hooper, stated that a near relative of Dr S— had cut off his hands, stabbed him to death, cut up his body and taken the pieces back to Iraq to show his family. The letter ended: 'We are all very sorry and are sure that he did not intend to do anything wrong, but it was just bad luck.'

Coulsdon and Purley Advertiser

A Lewes, Sussex Corporation clerk has been sentenced to 18 months imprisonment for stealing 14,000 new penny pieces from Eastbourne public lavatories. He spent the pennies on high living.

Irish Times

Climbing a churchyard memorial, James Kelly told P.C. Jeffrey Fish: 'I'm trying to get to God.'

'Surely there are other ways?' the Officer called up to him. In reply Kelly (33) let go his grip and crashed to the ground.

Southend Standard

On Tuesday for one day only there is a special presentation of the film of Jane Austen's *Pride and Prejudice* The story weaves its way through murder, anonymous phone calls, obscene letters and drug addiction to a deserted show-room in New York's rag trade district where the final drama is played out.

Enfield Gazette

A pot-luck dinner was held at the city park, one block north of the museum, as a fund-raising event to finance further repairs and improvements to Mrs Charles Seeger, museum committee Chairman.

Portland Oregonian

The water-soaked contents, which had lain in the metal chest for 50 years, were patted dry with paper towels and spread on a table for examination. Among these was Mrs Helen Lancing, who played the piano for the monument dedication 50 years ago.

New York State paper

'This is a quiet happy neighbourhood with dogs and children riding bicycles.'

Newsday

KENSINGTON PUBLIC LIBRARIES: 7.30 pm. English and csePiaLioo rsthe quick brown fox jump Landscape Painting in Oils.

Art News and Review

Clerk required for general duties in busy Streatham office. Ability to play the organ will be helpful.

Evening News

*   *   *

The prosecution alleged that Oseke Okeze, a 30-year-old herbalist, was asked by the deceased to prepare medicines that would make him bullet-proof. After administering the charm, the client demanded that it should be put to the test. The herbalist fired a shot at his customer who died on the spot, the court was told.

Manchester Evening News

A month ago, a 12-year-old boy was shot dead by a sentry on duty outside a fort in Lisbon. The sentry reported that the boy ignored his challenge in the dark. Army officials last night carried out a reconstruction of the events. A civilian, Carlos Chaves, aged 33, played the role of the boy. He too was shot dead.

Newcastle Chronicle

A 29-year-old man asked a Nottingham music shop owner: 'Do you sell square records?' Then he took off his jacket, grabbed a Bible from the counter and later assaulted two policemen.

Nottingham Post

*   *   *

Wanted urgently: Proficient drummer for Swindon-based trio. Plenty of work, reader/vocalist preferred, but nit essential.

Swindon Evening Advertizer

ACCOMMODATION WANTED
Young professional man
desires Bed-Sinningroom
for long period. Central.
Full board or without lunch.

Highland News

Intelligent young European lady wanted for interesting and responsible work. Typing useful but not essential. Must be proper good at grammer and spelling.

Foreign paper

Purchase tax on address book covers, stamp book holders, note book covers and similar receptacles will be chargeable at the rate of 6o per cent, unless they are merely plain folders having no means whatever of retaining the articles which they are designed to hold.

Customs Regulations

Inspector Venner said that following domestic trouble Mrs Kent and her husband had separated, and he had gone to live with his sister. On July 29 Mrs Kent went to see him, and while they were talking she pulled a small potato from her handbag and stabbed him. Fortunately the injury was not as serious as was at first thought.

Birkenhead News

Life as a bus driver is never dull. For instance, Mr Hagley recalls the day he ran over his conductor at Butterleigh.

Tiverton Gazette

TARANTULA – When a scientist dies in agony with his head swollen to twice its normal size and his hand grown claw-like, only Matt, the young town doctor, is suspicious.

Review in *Lincolnshire Free Press*

Centre-piece of the decorations was a huge cream urn behind the official table, filled with blue hydrangea and his wife; also some of the famous people who have stayed there including Dame Nellie Melba and Mark Twain.

Melbourne paper

HELP WANTED. Man wanted to handle dynamite. Must be able to travel unexpectedly.

Daily News, Newfoundland

Snell, out on the wing, held up United as they tried to push through on the right. Berry looked dangerous until Snell came on the scene, but he was eventually hundled over the liemla brelesatfetind wodatow line, ball as well.

Sunderland Echo

FOR SALE – Chromium plated revolting display Bottle Stand.

South African paper

GENTLEMEN and LADIES.

I am a *German* Surgeon, *&c.* who (being a Stranger here) am oblig'd to Publiſh Bills, therefore I muſt beg Pardon of the Publick if I do not expreſs my ſelf ſo well as others, for I do not deſign to make long Preambles and Tautologies; and I Scorn to Impoſe upon the World, let my Works ſpeak for me, and I give God the Glory. I Cure the following Diſtempers, if Curable, with all convenient Speed and Safety,

VIZ.

The Gravel, and Cut for the Stone,	The meaſles and Small Pox,
The Worms and the Cholick,	The Scurvy, and all Diſeaſes of the Eyes,
The Rickets and Ruptures in Children,	Wens without Cutting, and Sprains of the Back,
The Green Sickneſs,	The Astmah or Ptiſick.

And all other MALADIES

As I am a Surgeon, I Bleed in all Parts of the Body to Admiration, let the Patient be never ſo Young or Fat, if neceſſity requires. I likewiſe give my Advice in any Diſtemper, whether Curable or not, let it be ever ſo Occult or Chronick, which I will give under my Hand.

As for the Veneral Diſtemper, whether it be the Running of the Reins or a Confirm'd Pox, *&c.* I Cure it in as ſhort a time as the Caſe will admit, for I have had abundance of Experience Abroad in the Cure of it, therefore will not pretend to Patch it up.

(continued on page 93)

Mr Jensen described Faussett's pavilion as one of the many
'follies' typical of the 18th century. All sorts of miscel-
laneous antiquaries were hung around the walls.

Kent Messenger

A strong guest brought down a 112ft 70-ton blast furnace
stove in the Bilston, Staffordshire, iron and steel works.

Daily Mail

In dense fog the 7.43 am Strood (Kent) to Maidstone West
train crashed through the level-crossing gates at Aylesbury
(Bucks) but no one was hurt.

Portsmouth Evening News

NEW CITY COUNCIL
SETTLED DOWN WELL

Headline in *Auckland Star*

The man dropped the gramophone while running but the
policeman eventually caught him. It was stated defendant
had a record.

Belfast Telegraph

Inquire for *John Nevill*, at the Two *White Posts*, between the *Queen's Head* and the *White Lion*, over-againſt the *Union* Coffee-houſe at *Charing-Croſs*. My Hours are from Seven in the Morning till Ten, and from Seven till Nine in the Evening. I defire you would not ſlight this Method, but communicate this Bill to your Friends, becauſe I am a Stranger.

From the collection of 18th-Century
ephemera in the British Library

EIGHT Chrome Dining-room
CHAIRS, as new. Will split.
£9 each. Tel: Craddock 4964.

Advert in local paper

Other changes related to the agenda and included the decision to reduce the number of items by incorporating two items under the existing main heads. Thus 'Peaceful uses of nuclear energy' was placed under 'Economic co-operation' and 'mass destruction' under 'Promotion of Peace'.

Calcutta Statesman

Boy–C.S.M. Peter Henly, the winner of the Cassel silver medal for the best boy musician in the school, will play a corset solo during the concert.

East Kent Mercury

John Chapman of Hillview Road, Southborough, has
written to Southborough Council saying that the beacons
at the Charles Road crossing shine into his bedroom and
interfere with his sheep.

Kent and Sussex Courier

Ice-cream vendors, expecting big earnings in the next few
days, have arranged for huge socks to supply the city's
1,600,000 citizens.

Wolverhampton Express and Star

A still life oil painting by Pinxit fetched £1300 at a sale
conducted at the Hove Auction and Fine Art Galleries.

Sussex Express

When they went to Sheffield there was interference in every possible aspect of married life, including the cooking and upbringing of one of their sons, Bruce.

Evening News

Twenty-five specially made lightweight boxers, each lined with silver foil and containing 60lb of tinned and bottled foodstuffs, are being carried by rail from Nairobi to Mombassa today.

Tanganyika Standard

Crash courses are available for those wishing to learn to drive very quickly.

Advert in *Eastbourne Gazette*

A Channel tunnel will cut flying time to Paris from Heathrow by almost an hour, it was revealed last week.

Journal of Commerce

Ronnie Barker
Fletcher's Book of Rhyming Slang 80p

Get the brass tacks on what come out of the old north and south.

'Everybody has heard of rhyming slang. It dates back to time immoral. At least a hundred and fifty years, because the wife's mother doesn't remember it starting...' – says Ronnie Barker. He's put together a hilarious dictionary and phrase book of Cockney rhyming slang, ancient and modern, exactly as she is spoke. Take a butcher's!

compiled and edited by Robert Morley
illustrated by Geoffrey Dickinson and John Jensen
Robert Morley's Book of Bricks £1.25

The hilarious, bestselling collection of things people say – and then wish they hadn't...

'Whatever happened to that skinny blonde your husband was once married to?'
'I dyed my hair,' replied the lady.

A whole concert of clangers culled from everyone who will admit to brick-dropping.

All royalties donated to the National Society for Autistic Children.